Budget Burnout

*12 weeks to get out of your budget slump and
accelerate your goals*

Shay Richter

For information contact :

http://www.frontporchfinances.com

Book and Cover design by Kelsie Volker

First Edition: June 2023

CONTENTS

Introduction

I HAVE BEEN TIRELESSLY BUDGETING for six years, and while I actually like budgeting, sometimes life gets busy, and it can seem like a chore. I have found this to be true for myself and many other avid budgeters. After the birth of my first child, I had a fire in me to pay off debt. At the time I was newly married and had taken on about $45K in student loans (my husband's) while also having some debt of my own. I desperately wanted to become a stay-at-home parent. There was only one way I could make that possible, and that was to become debt-free. I created budget after budget, month after month. I picked up a side hustle to make some extra cash. We ate food that was on sale or discounted and I said "no" to going out with friends more often than not. During this time, I had to make budgeting interesting for me to keep up with my motivation.

After fifteen months of hard work and determination, we

became debt-free. Two weeks later, I was pregnant with our second child. I remember a complete feeling of relief when we found out. My oldest at the time was one and a half, and now I was going to be a mom again. I wanted to cry tears of joy. I was so happy. My children's lives would not be anything like mine growing up. Money was always tight when I was a kid. I always had everything I needed but not too much extra. My parents worked full time and were divorced. I don't have a ton of memories of my mom growing up and it's because she was working a lot. This led me to my goal of wanting to be a stay-at-home parent. I knew right then our lives would be forever changed by this single huge accomplishment. One week before my second baby was born, I quit my job and have been a stay-at-home working mom ever since. It was the greatest relief to do what I had always dreamed of doing and to feel financially secure doing it. There is real freedom knowing I could walk away from my career without putting extra stress or burden on my family.

Since becoming debt-free, my family has had other big financial goals. My husband and I want to retire by the age of forty and are currently on track to accomplish this by the time I am thirty-eight. One question I get asked often is *How do you stay motivated?* I am a very competitive person, and my greatest competition is usually myself. When I make a goal for myself, I typically will work hard to accomplish the challenge. I have created numerous money challenges for myself to keep me motivated through the years, some lasting weeks and others lasting years. I have done two year-long challenges that were difficult. In 2020 I did a "no buying new clothes" challenge, and in

2021 I did a no-buy challenge. These challenges are what led me to writing this book. Budget Burnout is a book about challenging yourself, to keep you motivated, on your toes, and to do these challenges in a short period of time.

Now don't worry, none of these challenges are year-long challenges. All of them are designed to last one week, but feel free to stretch them out longer or repeat. One of the hardest parts about working toward a long-term financial goal is motivation. How do you keep the excitement going week after week, month and month, and year after year? I understand that not everyone has the same personality as me to keep a year-long commitment to myself, and that is why these challenges are just small bites. It is difficult to be motivated for an entire year, but can you be motivated for twelve weeks?! These challenges or burnouts are designed to do just that! They will keep you motivated on whatever financial goal you may have. Can you give yourself twelve weeks to really push the envelope? To challenge yourself into new thinking and to step up with action and purpose to reach your goals?

I named this book *Budget Burnout* because I believe very much the repetitive nature of budgeting monthly can cause you to feel burnt out. Sometimes you need that extra motivation to remember the benefits of why you budget every month. The burnout in Budget Burnout also takes on a second meaning. If you like to work out, you know that a burnout set is where you exercise a muscle group till exhaustion. These sets will help you see some real progress in the gym. This book will do just that. It will push you till exhaustion to see real results. The meaning really can go both ways for this book. Give yourself just these 12 weeks and you will see real trackable progress and these challenges are set up to do just that.

A prerequisite to this book is you already need to be a budgeter. You need to know where your money is going and how much you spend each month on specific budget categories. How much do you spend monthly on groceries? Eating out? Etc. This is important because by knowing these numbers it will help you gauge an accurate amount of money to set aside towards your goal.

Let's Get Down to Business

AS I STATED BEFORE, YOU need to already have a budget to start this book and to complete the Burnouts. If you don't have one, today is the perfect time to start! Come back to this book in one to three months, and I will be here ready to challenge you!

Next, you need to have a goal. Is it to pay off debt? Save a large amount of money? Find more money for investing? Buy a new car? Money for Christmas? The money goals are endless. Tailor them to what your current money needs are. Write down your money goal on the goal sheet located at frontporchfinances.com/burnout/. When making your goal, here are a few things to keep in mind:

1. Make the goal challenging. Don't make it so simple that you can accomplish it in one week because we are working with twelve beautiful weeks. But, also, don't set the bar so high that you will never accomplish this goal.

2. Make your goal specific. Say you want to save $600 for the entirety of the book. Since there are twelve Burnouts, your goal would be $50 per week. Maybe some weeks you save more and some less, overall, this amount will keep you on track.

3. Make your goal time sensitive. This one is a little easier because it is just the duration of this book.

If you have heard of SMART goals before, these steps pretty much check all the boxes. The reason that a goal is required while reading this book is because having a goal in mind adds extra motivation to these challenges and reminds you what you are working toward.

While working through the Burnouts, some will be more time consuming than others. I suggest right after reading each Burnout, plan your week. You may have to give up a few hours of TV or phone time some weeks. Other weeks will require minimal planning and can be accomplished easily. Block out time in your week to get the tasks done! This is key to being successful! If you are more motivated in the morning, perfect, plan out your time in the mornings when you are focused. Really be realistic with your time.

A crucial part of this book is to have your budget done before you read the Burnout. You do not want to alter your budget for these challenges. The reason for not altering your budget is to gauge an accurate amount to put towards your money goal at the end of the week.

In each chapter, you will have a weekly Burnout challenge. If you are feeling up to it, you can adjust each of these to last two weeks to even a month depending on how motivated you are. This book is full of different tasks to keep you engaged in your money goals and to help you get creative on ways to save and make money. You can even do this book with a friend if you really want to get competitive. These Burnouts are designed to motivate you into new ways of thinking, shopping, and living. By extending the challenges longer than a week, you may even create some new healthy money habits.

At the end of all the Burnout challenges, you will see real numbers of just how much money went to your financial goal. How much can you save just by changing your mindset! Some weeks may only be twenty dollars and some may be hundreds. This isn't a get-rich-quick book; this is a book of endurance, planning, and hard work to push yourself to get to your goals quicker while having more fun.

1

I'M NOT MARRIED TO ANY OF THIS

IF THERE IS ONE THING I have learned since I became hyper focused on personal finance, it's that I will not stay with a company if I can find the same service for cheaper. Every year around the same time, for me it's around Christmastime, I start to dread checking the mail just knowing my auto insurance renewal is coming. You go out and get the mail every day, and then you finally get the bill. It's always nerve-wracking opening my car insurance bill. Will my premium stay the same, or do I need to come up with $200 by next week? Well, it just so happens that this year, my bill came on a cold December day. The kids and I bundled up and made the trip to the mailbox. My oldest at the time was two and her little sister was about six months. The kids have always loved going to the mailbox. It's always an adventure to see what awaits.

Once we were back home, I saw I received the piece of mail from my current auto insurance company. Always right on time! I sat down to open it hoping this year it's going to tell me, "Surprise, your premium is staying the same." Well, this was not what I saw. Our payment rose from $130 a month to $190 a month. Ouch. The thing about auto insurance companies is they never give you an actual reason why. I have gone to my insurance office and actually asked, and there isn't a specific reason. It's not like I had any tickets, new vehicles, or a recent accident. Nothing had changed, which is super frustrating. If anything, I should get a discount for another year of being a good driver!

Anyhow, I have never been super loyal to big corporations. Honestly, I just don't feel that I matter much to them. After talking to my insurance agent, I became a woman on a mission. I wasn't going to pay $60 more a month or an extra $720 a year for no reason. That is crazy, especially with the money goals we were working toward. The next day, I got on the phone. I searched for some companies that shop around for insurance. This is great because you can get multiple quotes at once. I made sure to keep everything the same as far as insurance coverage goes. I like to see the side-by-side comparison of the policies. After about a day, I was ready to switch. You may be thinking, *Shay, that seems like a lot of work and time.* Yes. Yes, it is!

After I received my quotes, I found one that would give me substantial savings if I paid for six months at a time. Luckily, I had some money in savings and decided this would be the best way to spend it! My payment went from $190 per month or $2,280 a year to $550 every six months or $1,100 a year. Savings of over $1,100 in one year! Yes, I had done it! I stuck it to the man—or at least the auto insurance company.

The Burnout

This week, your challenge is a daunting one. You will probably lose your patience and your mind. You must lower one bill. This bill could be the internet bill that has recently gone from $32.99 to $69.99. It could be getting rid of something on your cell phone bill that you don't use. It may be switching from one company to another because it's substantially cheaper. Maybe you're ready for a cheaper cell phone plan, internet, insurance, etc. Once you have completed this challenge, set aside the difference! Add the money to your goal.

2

Change in My Life

WHILE I WAS WORKING ON paying off debt, I was super strict with my budget. There was no need for extras; I had to put all the extra money towards debt. But every once in a while, I craved a take-out coffee. Making coffee at home is great and all, but I wanted that hit of dopamine. And a sugary coffee, let's be honest, is better than what I was making. My go-to during this time in my life was to round up all my loose change and use it to get a coffee. Fast-forward almost four years later, and I am still finding ways to get inexpensive coffee.

Recently, I decided to challenge myself to find all the change I could around my house. This wasn't a pre-planned task, just something I came up with that day. I really wanted an iced coffee from my local coffee shop! I told the kids what the plan was, and we went around the entire house and the cars looking for any and all change. The kids were eager and excited that I asked them to help with this task.

The first place we checked was the car, and let me tell you, there was money to be found. I have a little change holder, like most cars, and it was bursting at the seams. My little ones also found change on the floor, the center console, and in one of their cupholders. After we felt satisfied with what we found in the car, we decided to tackle the house.

Now with two small kids, ages five and three, my husband and I have become accustomed to not leaving any change lying around. Small change and small people do not mix. It's a nice habit we have had for the last five years. So, the kids and I had to think more creatively. Change in the couch? Nope. I do know that I am notorious for leaving money in pockets, usually jackets, especially during yard sale season (that time from April to October where I spend every Saturday buying second-hand treasures). At least once a year I will take out a jacket that I used the previous year and find cash and sometimes change. So, I decided this was the next place to check, and what do you know? I found change in my rain jacket and a corduroy jacket from last year.

Feeling good from all my finds, I then turned to the most obvious place to look, which was my purse and wallet. Definitely found another three to five dollars just there. At this point, I felt like I was running out of places to look. As the kids and I slowly walked through the house, we reached the laundry room. We found two quarters and a penny on top of the dryer. SCORE!

Now that we felt good about all the money we found, it was time to count all the change up. I let the kids help. It was the perfect time to practice some sorting skills and a learning opportunity to chat about the value of money. When all was said and done, we had found $20.81. I let the kids have all the pennies for their banks and gave them each a couple quarters for their help. They were elated. Overall, I had surpassed my goal to buy a coffee!

The Burnout

Spend the next seven days, or maybe just one if you want to block out some time, looking around the house and scooping up all that money lying around. This task is a pretty simple one, but don't for one second think it's any less important than the other challenges in this book. After finding all the change, count all of it up and add it to your money saving sheet. *Remember, it all adds up!*

3

Starting New Traditions

I USE TO HAVE THIS tradition where every New Year's Eve, after I got off work from working a large New Year's Eve event, I would come home exhausted, and suddenly I would get a second wind and have the urge to spend the next hour or so organizing my pantry. I don't know why I started doing this. Maybe it was to get my mind off the fact that I was too tired to get dressed up and go out with friends or just that I wanted to start the new year fresh. I would get home and start taking everything out of my ridiculously small pantry that doubled as my laundry room. By the end, I was throwing out so much food that had expired.

Once we started paying off our debt and becoming more money conscious, I tried to only buy food I knew we would eat. I also learned that food waste is a huge problem in the United States. Our food waste was cut down drastically at that point! I was actively looking out for food in my fridge and pantry about to expire. So now, instead of organizing my pantry once a year, I was organizing it multiple times per year and consciously making recipes from what I had on hand.

I love eating food and cooking for my family. We now have a large garden that we eat from all summer long, and I also try to preserve as much food as I can to eat during the winter months. Our garden is a huge food-money saver for us. Every spring, I usually do a whole month where I focus on using the food we have at home and spend minimally at the grocery store. I do this for a few reasons: first, it allows me to go through what we have and eat up anything that is about to expire (I can also see what foods we aren't eating and know not to purchase those anymore). Second, I can get through the rest of our food from last year's harvest, to make room for the current year's garden produce. Third, it allows me to gain control of my grocery budget and come in substantially under budget.

Spring 2022 was no different. After spending $1,000 the previous month on groceries, I knew it was time to utilize what we had on hand and spend money only on perishables each week. Also note, 2022 was a year where inflation had hit most Americans hard, and the high grocery prices were just killing my budget.

Let me tell you, when I do pantry challenges, my recipes get weird. I substitute the most random items in recipes just to stretch my food even further. I even stole a few bags of chips from my dad's house just to get through the rest of the month. And yes, I eventually bought him some chips to replace the bags I had taken. By the end of the month, my husband was probably tired of all the weird stuff we were eating, but when I ran the numbers at the end of April that month, we only spent $252.96, which was astronomically less than the previous month! The best part was my pantry and freezer had plenty of space for the upcoming harvest.

The Burnout

For one week, eat up the food you already have on hand in your pantry, fridge, and freezer. Do an inventory of what you have. Check expiration dates and eat anything about to expire. There are many websites that let you put in ingredients and will tell you recipes you can make from them. Do not be afraid to get creative and try something new. As some fresh items are needed, try not to spend over $25 for the week at the grocery store. Take your weekly grocery budget minus what you spent at the grocery store to get the amount to add to your "savings sheet" for the week.

You can calculate your weekly food budget by taking your regular food budget total for the month and dividing it by the number of days in that month. Then multiply that number by seven. That is how much you would typically spend in a week on groceries. The key to this challenge is not to overspend the next week. Keep your spending as usual. Anytime you feel the need, repeat this challenge. This burnout can be done once a month or quarter. Plus, you can stretch it longer if you really want a save some money!

4

This Was Planned

I AM A PLANNER. I plan out vacations down to what we are doing and where/what we are eating each day. I plan out large and small purchases that need to be made, sometimes starting to save a year or more in advance. I do this to save money and to create less stress. I can usually find what I need and spend a fraction of the amount most people spend, all while not feeling pressured to buy. We need a new roof. The roof is a current goal we are working toward, and this goal will take us about three years to fully save for. Planning purchases keeps you from breaking your budget, and sometimes you can even find things on sale because you have planned so far in advance.

I am also a big proponent of purchasing second-hand. Not

just because it is great for the environment but because purchasing secondhand can, and has, saved me massive amounts money. I can count on two hands all the brand-new clothes and shoes I have purchased for my family of four in the last three years. I always shop second-hand first. I do the same with furniture (which is stupid expensive brand-new) and especially household items.

In our house, we have three bedrooms. Two of the three bedrooms are especially large. At around two years old, we transitioned my youngest into a toddler bed. With her being the youngest, she naturally had the smallest room, well, because she was the smallest. Her room accommodated the crib just fine, but anything larger and she would have practically no space while my oldest was swimming in the space she had. The big room is about twice the size of the small room. We decided we would put them in the same room and get bunk beds. I grew up sharing a room with my two sisters, and it taught me a lot. Our room was small. We had a bunk bed and a futon. Remember futons? Those things were so uncomfortable.

My husband and I decided how much we would save up for the bunk beds and what kind of bunk beds we were looking for. Looking online, cheap bunk beds brand-new we liked were $900, and the quality looked questionable. Now, we could afford that by setting aside money for a few months, but I wanted something a little more high quality. Honestly, a $900 bunk bed would be the most expensive piece of furniture in our home. We really wanted bunk beds that were multipurpose. We decided we wanted a bunk bed that had built-in storage, so the girls' room didn't have to have two mismatched dressers taking up space. It would be extremely hard to find two second-hand dressers that looked the same.

While we were saving for the beds, I was scouring Craigslist, Facebook Marketplace, and my local Facebook Buy Nothing page. One day, I found a set on Facebook that looked great. The set had the dresser, a built-in desk, and a bookshelf, and it just was listed for $300. I looked up some comparable bunk beds on Facebook Marketplace and other people wanted $600 to $1,000 for the same used bunk beds. I looked up the retail price online, and they sell for over $2K. I knew we had to jump on this deal. I contacted the owner, and we picked them up later that evening. The best part is the bunk beds are way nicer quality than what we would have been able to buy brand-new. When you are not in a rush to buy it takes off a lot of stress. Preplanning for large purchases can allow you to score great deals!

The Burnout

What is something you have been saving for, big or small? The challenge for this week is to find that item used (in great condition). Buy it and save the difference. So, if you saved $1,000 for a piece of furniture and found it used for $500, you would save the difference of $500. That amount would go toward your money goal!

5

Do Not Swipe That Debit Card (To Swipe or Not to Swipe)

THE YEAR OF 2021, I embarked on a no-spend year. While this week's challenge will be wildly different, it will have the same purpose. Now, for my no-spend year, I made up a list of rules that I had to follow. I couldn't spend money on eating out, home decor, clothing, but I could spend money on items for my garden and vacations with my family. My rules were really a reconstruction of how we used our money. I cut out all the junk and just kept what was important to us as a family. The nourishment of my family and great experiences are what I find important to spend my money on. I could of course use money for essentials like food and household items as part of my challenge.

Doing a no-spend year takes creativity. One area I found the easiest was gift giving. Most people spend too much on gifts, and let's be honest, many of them aren't utilized and end up being donated or tossed. I grew chamomile, dried the flowers and gave it as teacher gifts and gifts to friends. We also grew cut flowers. Handpicked bouquets always go over well for gifts. During the holiday season, we baked gifts. I really think our friends and family enjoyed that we took time to bake treats.

I did fail three of the twelve months on this challenge, but I also succeeded for nine months. By the end of the year, we had invested an extra $15K into our brokerage account and put $8K into home repairs (2021 was the year it seemed like everything was breaking). We saved/invested 43% of our income just by not buying random items at Target or going to Chipotle two times a week. It was wild how much we saved. Now that we are in 2023, I still hold on to what we learned from that year, but I am not as strict. I am a firm believer that sometimes you have to grind and other times you get to coast. Everyone can easily feel burnt out quickly when they are depriving themselves all of the time. For me I easily get burnt out when I don't have cash for experiences, travel, or thrifting money.

The Burnout

The challenge that lies ahead of you this week is going to be a doozy. Your goal is to spend $0. You can still pay your bills but buy nothing else. No eating out, grocery shopping, etc. Do not swipe that debit or credit card. Let no money leave your accounts. At the end of the week, take all the money you have saved and add it to your money goal! Don't forget to fill out your sheet! Do not do this challenge when you know you have something pressing where money will need to be spent. This challenge will 100% test your willpower. This may be one of the biggest money-saving weeks. Do not overspend the week before or after!

Shay Richter

6

You Got That for Free?

"YOU GOT THAT FOR FREE?" I hear this phrase all the time. I like— no, wait, *I love*—free stuff! Right toward the beginning of the pandemic, I learned about Buy Nothing groups. These are groups on Facebook in different areas all over the world. Currently there are groups in over forty countries. So, in March 2020, I joined my local Buy Nothing group. A Buy Nothing group is an online group page, usually on Facebook, where people give away items for free. I can't tell you how many items I have posted on there. Especially items my youngest has grown out of. I have seen all sorts of things given away for free from food, furniture, gifts of service, etc.

During my no-buy year the Buy Nothing group came in handy for Christmas and birthday gifts. I have received end tables, a couch with a hide-a-bed and new mattress, spice rack, toddler hiking backpack we took to Zion National Park, shelves, artwork, snowsuits, puzzles, Instant Pot, and so much more. The community is so wonderful. I also love giving in return.

When both of my girls were big enough, we knew we wanted to get them a play structure. Not a small playground, one of the large ones with a big slide. Looking online, we found them for about $1,200 for a brand-new one. After my husband and I discussed it, we budgeted $600 to buy one used off Marketplace. Just for kicks and giggles, I asked my Buy Nothing group if anyone had a play structure they wanted to get rid of. I specifically posted that we would move it because we all know it's not easy to move those. Not even an hour later, a single mom replied and sent me a picture of what she had. Her play structure was way nicer than what I expected. The playground was there when she moved into her house and her kids were too old to play on it. She wanted to put a large shed where it was. So, it ended up working out great for her also. It took three truckloads of to get it over to our house. My husband sanded all the wood, and we used some leftover outdoor paint from another project. Overall, we spent $0 of our $600 budget!

The Burnout

Find something for free. Any item that you need or one you were budgeting to buy. The key word is *need*. You can trade with someone you know or join a free or Buy Nothing group. Get your free item and save the difference. For us, we were able to save $600, and we used it for investing.

7

You Have Food at Home

MY BROTHER-IN-LAW, TEO, and my sister, Kyshandra, really like to experiment in the kitchen. Teo and my Kyshandra lived with us for almost two years, and overall, Teo made a majority of our dinners. In 2020, I created a sourdough starter (surprise, surprise, sourdough starters were a real trend during the pandemic). Teo learned to make all sorts of breads out of it. His pretzels were especially good. When Teo said he was making pizza, you knew you were in for an evening of many crazy-delicious pizzas. My sister would make a sourdough crust and he would make a homemade sauce with garden tomatoes. The toppings he would add would include Kalamata olives, broccoli, eggplant, and whatever he could find in the garden or fridge. He would never make just one pizza; Teo's pizza nights sometimes included up to ten different pizzas.

During my no-buy year, we did not budget for eating out. We were treated by family a few times and sometimes my husband used his personal spending money to take us out. (During the no-buy year, I opted for no spending money while my husband still wanted his). It's easy to eat at home when you know you do not have any other options. Sometimes, I would splurge and buy a frozen pizza for the kids, but mostly we ate delicious homemade meals. I am not going to pretend to take credit for most of these meals. Teo made a great deal of these dinners. We would collaborate on the meal plan for the week so I could do the grocery shopping and he was typically the person who executed these meals.

The Burnout

Get a sense of what you have around your house in the fridge, pantry, and freezer because your challenge this week is to not eat out. This will take a bit of planning and preparation. You will need to account for days when you may not have the time to make dinner. On those days, you will need to have a meal ready that is easy to make or leftovers from the night before, but overall, preparation is key. Make sure to have groceries on hand to pack for lunches or snacks to bring while out and about. By having quick easy food on-hand you are less tempted to buy something on the go. Take whatever money you typically have budgeted for eating out and send it straight to your savings. Also, do *not* blow your grocery budget for the week! The idea is to utilize the forgotten pantry item or food hidden in the back of the fridge or freezer!

Shay Richter

8

Less Is More

YOU KNOW THAT FEELING YOU get when you look around your room when it's clean and decluttered and all is right in the world? When my husband and I started paying off debt, we sold a lot of our own stuff. Anything that wasn't needed was gone. After that, we felt amazing. We had made some quick cash and opened up more space for our family to grow in our home. It made cleaning easier and helped with our mindset of what we brought into our home.

After our youngest grew out of her crib, I had the itch to sell. I am not one to hold onto too much stuff for sentimental reasons. I have pictures and memories. I also like to leverage selling items to purchase new items. We try to take care of the things in our home to the best of our ability as a family with two young kids. This crib was one of the only brand-new furniture pieces in our house, and it was time to move on. We wanted to use that money to get our girls a nice, gently used, bunk bed.

I don't mess around when I post things for sale. I list them for a reasonable price, and I am sure to include all flaws because I don't want to waste people's time. After looking at what other cribs were selling for, I listed mine for $75. We had purchased it four years prior for $115. Within two days, the crib sold.

The cost of that crib we had for four years and used with our two babies was $40. I would say that is pretty good. We then were able to roll that money into a solid wood bunk bed that houses a lot of storage for $300. We do this often with things our family outgrows. I try and buy quality items that can resell for a decent amount. Then we can use that money to buy another quality item and it starts a snowball effect.

One of the best ways to meet your money goals quickly is to sell unused items from around your house. The additional money coming in helps to keep you motivated. It's money in your pocket and gives you a quick boost to keep going.

The Burnout

This week your focus is to sell, sell, sell. Your goal is to make $100 in seven days selling things you no longer use or need around your home. It can be clothing, furniture, or other random home items. It can be one expensive item or twenty cheaper items.

Some places to list items for sale are Facebook Marketplace, OfferUp, Nextdoor app, Poshmark, and eBay. Add the money to your goal sheet as the items sell!

9

The Most Wonderful Time of the Year

DURING MY NO-BUY YEAR, I had to get creative in a multitude of ways. But especially during the holidays! How do I create a memorable and magical holiday for my kids while not spending exuberant amounts of money?!

Christmas was a little harder. When it came to decorating, we used the decor that we use every year. We have several types of pine trees outside. We clipped some branches to make some garland. We bake oranges in the oven and stringed them as decor. It really felt nice to spruce up the house with beautiful scents, and the kids enjoyed the festivities too!

There are quite a few free holiday activities near us. We saw a holiday light show that was set to music and found some free hot cocoa. We all danced and sang songs. My kids, still, to this day talk about this place. Of course, we had to go see Santa, and one thing I learned was that there are plenty of places that offer free Santa pictures, or you can take the photos on your phone for free. After a month of fun, free activities, decorating, and baking, I realized we didn't lack anything that we had in years prior, and I saved a bunch of money in the process.

The Burnout

In this week's challenge, you will need to get creative. Look to the next holiday, whether it's Halloween, Valentine's Day, Christmas, even someone's birthday, and do the holiday for free. Of course, make sure to have budgeted for the festivities beforehand so you know the specific amount that you will save. Some things to consider are decor, gifts, food, activities, or anything else you normally budget for. You got this!

10

Wait, I'm Paying for What?

"OOOH, THAT'S A GOOD DEAL." This is me as I am shopping for my vitamins and see they are 20% off. I am notorious for stocking up on everyday items I use. Whether it is food or household products. So, as I get ready to add to cart the three bottles of my multivitamin, I see I can get an extra 10% off if I get the subscription. *Perfect*, I think to myself. I can cancel the subscription as soon as they get here. Think of all of those extra savings I just received! Well, guess what? Surprise! I did not cancel the vitamins, and a month later I had six months' worth of vitamins, and the second month cost me substantially more. The kicker is, I didn't budget for it, and now I have to find where to pull that money from.

I would like to say this is the only time that has happened to me, but it isn't. Just recently, I went through my bank account and wrote down all my subscriptions. When most people think of subscriptions, they think of Spotify or Amazon and they don't take into account other forms of subscriptions like vitamins, toilet paper, coffee, etc. So, after going through my bank statements and emails (this is also super helpful when nailing down your subscriptions), I found three subscriptions to cancel: drink mixes, meat delivery, and car air fresheners. These three subscriptions totaled $121.63 per month. While I do like all these products, I didn't need them. We recently bought a half a cow, so we didn't need the meat box anymore. I already have too many car air fresheners piling up, and I stocked up on the drink mixes when they were on sale. This is a savings of $1,459 per year! All because I took one hour to go through my subscriptions to see what I needed and what I don't need. I still have many other subscriptions, but I canceled the ones that weren't serving me anymore.

The Burnout

This week's challenge is simple but will take a little time. Carve out at least an hour to complete this task. Go through your bank statements and emails. Write down every subscription you have. Don't forget to check place like Amazon and even your phone for apps you pay for monthly or even yearly. For your list, write down the subscriptions and the cost associated with them. Go through each subscription and think about how it is serving your life. Do you *need* it? Does it bring you joy? Did you forget to cancel it? Or was the subscription a spur-of-the-moment buy? Pick at least one subscription to cancel, but the more the better. Take that monthly amount and add the money to your goal! The best part of this challenge is you will be saving money every month!

Shay Richter

11

It's Time to Let Go

WHEN I FIRST STARTED WORKING hard to become debt-free in July 2017, I had a fire in me. By August, I had decided it was time to sell stuff. Little of what I owned then or even now is of great importance to me. I rounded up all the random stuff I could find. I needed to put a dent in this debt I had, which at the time was a car, my husband's student loans, and a personal loan for our heat pump totaling about $57K.

As I scoured the house, my mother-in-law came to me and said she was going through some boxes from storage. If I helped her organize them, I could sell whatever she didn't want to keep. The next day I packed up my almost six-month-old and headed to her house. As I sorted, I looked up some comparable items on eBay, curious of the values. I categorized everything, packed the boxes up in my car, and headed home.

In just a few days, I was going to set out everything for a yard sale. I had tables put up in my garage and started placing things out and pricing them. By Friday, it was go time! I invited some other family members to bring anything they wanted to sell just to make the yard sale larger and more appealing.

By the end of the weekend, we donated anything I didn't want to sell online. I added up all my cash, and I made $360. I know this isn't a huge amount, but this was about what I made at my job per week. I was working about twenty hours a week from home, so I didn't have to get child-care. This felt like a huge win. Less stuff in my house and more money to put toward debt.

Quite often on Instagram, I post about how paying off debt and minimalism go hand in hand. When you have that fire to pay off debt, you realize that the stuff in your home took your money and your time. In the moment you feel you *have* to have it, and then that item usually ends up in a closet somewhere six months later. Many people clear out their homes while paying off debt, getting rid of anything that doesn't serve their purpose. In return, they have less stuff, less cleaning, and less debt!

The Burnout

Guess what?! You are going to do a yard sale. You have one week to accomplish this. Get rid of anything you haven't used recently, don't remember ever owning, or that doesn't serve your life anymore. Here is a tip: do not price your items too high. Everyone thinks their stuff is worth what they bought purchased it for, and it just isn't. Price the items to sell, because whatever is left after the yard sale, you need to donate. Price the items like you want them gone! Add the money you make to your money sheet.

Shay Richter

12

I Am a Wannabe Foodie

I LOVE TO GO OUT, do fun activities, and of course try new restaurants. While my family is new to the whole vacation thing, since we didn't do much traveling while paying off debt, we only eat out about once per trip. This is just because eating out is so expensive. As a whole, my little family of four are not picky eaters. We love trying new foods. Yes, even the three-year-old is adventurous with her palette. When I mentioned to my husband that I wanted to do a no-buy year, it took him a few days to get on board because this meant getting rid of our eating-out budget. At the time, we budgeted $100 per month.

Now you are probably wondering, *how did you go a whole*

year without eating out? Short answer: we didn't. I used cash-back apps to cash out money from many different sites. My Ibotta had almost $100 in it before I cashed out. I determined this was a loophole because this money isn't part of our income. In the no-buy year, my husband didn't want to give up his monthly spending money, which was fine. After all, this whole crazy idea was mine, but what that meant was he got to choose if he wanted to spend his money at restaurants. We had some fun date nights that reminded me of back when we were dating since he was using "his money" to pay for the date. Overall, we didn't go out to eat that many times during the year, and we were able to save a bunch of money because of it.

Currently it has been two years since our no-spend year, and surprisingly, we still don't have an "eating out" line item in our budget. We still use cash back, gift cards, and our personal spending money. However, we do have a date night line item, which can be used for food, but we prefer activities. One of my 2022 goals was to have a date night once every month, and we have continued this in 2023.

The Burnout

How much do you spend on eating out per month? Per week? This week's challenge is probably everyone's least favorite. Do not go out to eat for an entire week unless you have a free way to do so. This challenge is remarkably similar to the eating-at-home challenge. The only difference is you can get creative by using cash-back apps or gift cards to go out to eat if necessary. Take some time to plan your week and your meals to make this more successful. At the end of that week, put your money toward your goal!

Conclusion

YOU DID IT! YOU HAVE finished the whole twelve weeks! How did you do?! Are there some challenges you want to do again? The best part about this book is that you can come back to it again and again and save money every time. My hope for you now that you have finished the book is you are even closer to your current money goals. I have seen great strides in myself from doing these challenges. I was really able to accelerate my own personal money journey by constantly challenging myself. Now that you have finished, know that it's important to spend a while going back to your normal budget. After you have had a good rest come back and do these burnouts again!

Shay Richter

Printed in Great Britain
by Amazon

24200697R00036